CYBER SECURITY SIX PACK™

IMPROVING YOUR CYBER SECURITY AND PRIVACY IN SIX SIMPLE STEPS

2nd Edition

JAMES PATTERSON "PAT" WICKS

Columbus, GA

Tidan Publishing LLC
P.O. Box 9482
Columbus, Georgia 31907
Tidanpublishingllc@gmail.com

Distributed by Tidan Publishing LLC
Cover Design & Illustrations by Obsidian Lewin-Holmes,
Gina Bonanno, James Patterson "Pat" Wicks and Tidan Publishing

Published 2022
Columbus, Georgia
Printed in the United States of America
ISBN 978-1-7368173-1-5
ISBN 978-1-7368173-4-6 (2nd Edition)

DEDICATION

I dedicate this book to my family and friends that are like family:

My wife Alyssa, who loves me despite my flaws and supports me in all of my endeavors.

My children J.P. and Chara, who keep me centered and give my life purpose.

My late father, Vernon (Pete), who recognized and cultivated my talent for technology before I realized it for myself.

My mother, Jeannette, the inspiration for this book, encouraged me to speak with people about computers at their level rather than telling them what to do.

To my Four Stars – Tammy, Lonnie, Pam, and Alicia, who provide sound counsel and hold me accountable.

To my brother, my sisters, and my dozens of in-laws, aunts, uncles, nieces, nephews, cousins, and friends that motivate me to be a better man every day.

To my contributing editors: Linda Duncan, Jonathan Chow, Beau Canada, and my wife Alyssa.

TABLE OF CONTENTS

CYBER SECURITY AND PRIVACY FOR EVERYONE

Cyber security is a branch of information technology that can be incredibly complex, but it can be much simpler when dealing with your personal devices and networks. It helps to think about cyber security in the same manner that you think about physical security. The physical security requirements for protecting a military base that houses nuclear weapons are incredibly complex. By comparison, the physical security requirements for protecting your home are incredibly simple. When protecting the people and property in your home, you may have deadbolt locks, security cameras, or security fences securing your property. You do this to make your home the harder target, more resistant to attack from criminals. Hard targets encourage attackers to go elsewhere to commit their crimes. The same "hard target" principles should apply to personal cyber security.

We all want to make our computers, smartphones, and online accounts harder targets to encourage criminal hackers to go elsewhere to commit their malicious activity. We also want to better protect our privacy. Applying the techniques in this book can help you become a harder target. While it requires a little planning and commitment, it's not rocket science.

I like to use examples of physical security to explain cyber security and privacy concepts. Most people understand the need to take a few extra steps to protect their home or car. When you compare protecting a computer to protecting a car, the concepts are easier to understand. For example, some people like to use the same email address and password for all of their online accounts. These "keys" to your accounts are just like the keys to your home, car, garage, office, storage unit, and bank safe deposit box. Would you use one key for all of those? Of course not. Just like your home and car require unique keys, your online accounts require unique passwords/passphrases. Just like it takes a little effort to protect your home and car, implementing effective cyber security and privacy practices for your computer and smartphone takes a little effort as well.

Before we delve deep into the techniques to implement effective cyber security, we must first look a little deeper into the topic of cyber security itself. Let's start with acknowledging a few hard facts:

- No computer, operating system, or application is hack-proof - period!

- If your computer or smartphone is on a network, it is susceptible to hacking.

- Even the most secure computers and devices can be hacked when unsafe practices are used.

Brilliant people create computers, smartphones, tablets, smartwatches, personal assistants, operating systems, and the applications that run on them. Other clever people work hard to hack these items for intelligence, profit, and destruction. It's a constant arms race - criminal hackers try to poke holes in hardware and software devices, and creators patch the holes they find as quickly as possible. The only thing that we, as users of these technologies can do is keep up with the patches as they become available. More on that later.

When your digital devices are on your home network or on the internet, they are susceptible to hacking. This includes your smartphones, tablets, or computers. A personal assistant, a security camera, an alarm system, and the controls to a water treatment system are all susceptible to hacking. The only way to lessen the likelihood of an electronic device being hacked on a network is to implement solid security practices. Most governments, businesses, and schools have pretty good corporate device security. We will go over a few tips to enhance your personal device security and increase your protective posture when you are away from home.

Unfortunately, many hacks occur when people use their devices in an unsafe manner. Sometimes, misuse is intentional, like installing software from sketchy websites to save a few dollars. Other times the misuse is unintentional, like failing to update an app that was installed some time ago. Companies have suffered breaches after delaying the installation of a security patch. Introducing new habits to replace these unsafe practices is one of the focuses of this book.

When speaking to different people about the importance of cyber security, I often hear the statement " Hackers don't care about me because I don't have anything important to steal." These people are partially right in their assertions. In general, criminal hackers don't care about you personally. They don't know you from the next person when they go out to steal information. You are just an email account and password that they can now exploit to gain access to additional information which they can use, sell or ransom. That's because information is the lifeblood of the Internet. Information equals money. It's the new gold, it's the new oil, and we must understand how our information is being used so that we can protect it properly.

Many of the services used on the Internet are free to use – that is, you do not pay an obvious fee for the service. Popular services like Google, Facebook, Instagram, Snapchat, LinkedIn and Twitter do not charge an up-front fee to use their sites. So how do companies like Google and Facebook generate billions of dollars in revenue each year? They sell your information, of course! To paraphrase a popular phrase – "If you are not paying for a product, you are the product that is being sold." Your posts, likes, dislikes, interests, and the sites you visit are collected and this information is sold to advertisers. Even if you don't think your information is not important, these online companies know better.

Bottom line – nothing is hack proof. Your information has value and unscrupulous people will try to steal your information. Not to worry though, protecting your privacy and improving your cyber security are the primary goals of this book. With a little effort, you can make your devices harder targets. Again, not rocket science. the *Cyber Security Six Pack* ™ is designed to strengthen your security, tighten up your personal cyber security practices, and expand your knowledge when operating on the Internet.

HACKERS, THEIR TOOLS, AND THEIR TECHNIQUES

It is important to note that not all hackers are criminals. The media and motion picture industry has misused the term "hacker" so much that the mere mention of the word creates images of hooded narcissists sitting in a basement, wreaking havoc on society. A hacker is simply someone that uses a computing device in a manner not intended by the device's creator. If you boost the speed of your computer above the intended speed, that's a hack. Not all hacking is criminal, and if you hack your own computing devices, you are not breaking the law. If someone gains unauthorized access to computing systems or exceeds the privileges they have on a system, they can be classified as criminal hackers.

Depending on which list you choose to use, there are up to

ten types of "hackers." However, I will just focus on the following three:

Bad Actors - Criminal hackers who attack for financial gain, foreign governments, competitive advantage, political advocacy, or just plain destructive purposes. Bad actors can also be malicious employees that attack companies from the inside, neighbors that steal your Wi-Fi, or a vengeful "ex" that wants to harm you electronically.

Security Researchers - Cyber specialists that look for flaws in electronic systems and responsibly report their findings to companies for patching. While some people object to the activities of security researchers, they play an important role in keeping our systems and networks safe.

Cyber Security Professionals - Cyber specialists who protect the companies or governments they work for by attacking their own systems to discover vulnerabilities before the bad actors do. The five primary areas of expertise for cyber security professionals are:

> **Application Security Specialist:** Cyber security software developers that look for flaws in apps and fix them before the software is exploited.

> **Network Defenders:** Network engineers that monitor and protect networks for unauthorized or malicious activity and intrusions.

Incident Responders: Cyber professionals that act to stop the attack whenever malicious activity is detected. They also perform forensic examinations to determine the cause of the attack, and help to return the systems to normal operation.

System Defenders: Engineers that focus on hardening operating systems against attack and deploy systems to maintain the security and integrity for all digital devices on the network.

Governance, Compliance and Risk Teams: These professionals know the legal and regulatory cyber security requirements for their business, then develop standards for the business to follow and measure compliance with the standard that have been set.

Criminal hackers understand people are creatures of habit. If the criminal hackers can get your email address and password for one website such as Gmail, chances are that the same username and password will work on other websites. While there may be nothing of value in a Gmail account, abusing the Amazon or Bank of America accounts could be quite profitable. The criminals may also use the Gmail credentials to access your photos saved in "The Cloud" (aka, someone else's computer). If they find an image that you don't want to share with the public, the criminal hackers may blackmail you into paying hush money to prevent them from sending the image to everyone on your contact list.

Criminal hackers can gain unauthorized access to our systems and personal information using various techniques. Here are a few malicious software (malware) terms to know before we talk about the techniques:

- **Virus** - Malicious computer code that can replicate and spread to other computers by attaching itself to other files and applications. When the other file is opened or executed, the virus activates.

- **Worm** - Code that reproduces and works independently of user action, jumping from device to device and network to network.

- **Ransomware** – Malicious code designed to encrypt data and block access to a computer system, device or network until a sum of money is paid.

- **Trojan Horse** – Trojan Horse code appears to do one thing, but contains hidden functionality that is activated after the code is added to a device.

- **Spyware** – Code capable of recording and reporting a user's actions without the user's explicit permission or knowledge. The individuals or companies receiving the information are not generally considered criminal hackers, just people profiting from the information they collect.

This is not a comprehensive list of all malware, just a few of the most common malware used to affect the general public. There are many types of malware that are important for you to protect your devices and systems. Your current protective software may safeguard against viruses and worms, but may not protect against ransomware.

Knowing what to protect against allows you to make better decisions when deciding which software best secures your devices.

Here are a few techniques used by the criminal hackers out there:

- **Phishing** – A criminal tries to trick someone into divulging information like usernames, email addresses, passwords, or credit card numbers by impersonating a trusted person in an email or direct message. When done through text messages or SMS, it is known as "smishing." The cliche "Prince whomever" just needs a few dollars of your money to get his full fortune is a good example of a phishing email.

- **Spoofing** – A bad actor successfully masquerades as another by falsifying data and thereby gaining unauthorized access to system or network. The impersonation can be the person themselves or the person's computer address (IP Address).

- **Brute Force Attack** - Criminal hackers use code to check all possible passwords until they find the correct one. The hackers use dictionaries and databases known as Rainbow Tables to break into accounts.

- **Drive-By Download** - Drive-by downloads are hacks that happen when unknowingly visiting an infected website, viewing an infected e-mail message or by clicking on a malicious pop-up window Just the simple act of viewing a web page or clicking a link could lead to an infection.

- **Man-in-the-Middle Attack** - Criminal hackers electronically place themselves in between a user on a device and their intended destination on the network or Internet. The hackers can copy, block or modify the user's communications, stealing passwords, credit cards and other sensitive data. Sometimes, the criminals actually redirect traffic to servers they control, fooling people into thinking that they are at their actual destination.

- **Sniffing** - This refers to the eavesdropping of electronic communications by criminal hackers. This differs slightly from the "Man-in-the-Middle" attack in that sniffing is a passive action only, capturing electronic communications but not blocking or modifying the communications. Sniffing can happen by someone using the same public Wi-Fi network (depending on the network's security level and hardware used).

- **Social Engineering Attack** - Criminals psychologically manipulate people into performing actions they would not perform or divulging confidential information. Whether by phone call, pop-up message, email or text, these criminals convince people to install software that allows them to control your computer or provide passwords or codes to access your accounts. Phishing, Smishing and Spoofing are also categorized as Social Engineering Attacks.

While it is important to know about the different types of attacks and malware used by criminal hackers, knowing how to protect yourself is more important. The practices in this book, the *Cyber Security Six Pack* ™, if implemented properly, will measurably reduce the likelihood of you being taken advantage of by the "bad actors" out there. These techniques will not stop every attack, since new attacks are emerging all the time. However, these techniques will give you a firm foundation of cyber security to make you a harder target, one that most "bad actors" will bypass in favor of easier prey!

THE CYBER SECURITY SIX PACK ™

The *Cyber Security Six Pack* ™ was developed to reduce the likelihood of a criminal hacker taking advantage of weak device security. As previously stated, no electronic device on a network is hack-proof. When a person becomes the victim of a criminal hacker, one of the first questions they ask is what did I do wrong. The truth of the matter is you can do everything right and still get hacked. There are two types of hacks that you can do little about:

> 1. **<u>Website holding your data is hacked</u>:** Hundreds of websites have been hacked over the years. Some people had their personal information (email address, password, home address, credit card number, etc.) stolen because a website they visited had poor security, or the site's administrators forgot to apply a security patch.

2. **Application and protocol abuse:** Some applications and protocols that run websites and network communications are decades old. From time to time, people identify flaws in these protocols and bad actors use that information to attack. Some people had their personal information stolen because of flaws in the software they were using. These flaws can be a gateway to encrypt information as it travels over the Internet.

As stated before, there is little that you as an individual can do to prevent this sort of hack. You can, however, prevent the kind of criminal hack that happens when a person does not practice sound cyber security practices. That is where this book comes in. There is an old joke that goes something like this:

Two friends are walking in the woods when they come across a huge, hungry-looking bear. At first, both friends freeze in their tracks. Then one friend slowly starts to stretch. Perplexed, the other friend says, "What are you doing? You cannot outrun a bear!" The first friend said, "I don't have to outrun the bear. I just have to outrun you!"

This book is designed to help you outrun the other people on the internet in terms of personal cyber security and privacy. The *Cyber Security Six Pack* ™ provides you with enough guidance to significantly increase your cyber protective posture, while not overwhelming you with geek talk and hundreds of acronyms.

So what will the *Cyber Security Six Pack* ™ do for you?

- **Your logins will be more secure!**
- **Your systems will be more secure!**
- **Your data will be more secure!**

Criminal hackers would prefer to steal data that is easy to obtain. They don't want to spend hours or days trying to break into a system with strong security or an encrypted file system. If a target is too hard, they move on to the next one. If you find yourself to be the individual target of a determined criminal hacker or state-sponsored group of bad actors–drop this book and call the police and the nearest FBI field office. The six components of the *Cyber Security Six Pack* ™ are:

- **Step I - Use Unique Passphrases and Multi-Factor Authentication for your Online Accounts**
- **Step II - Back Up Your Computers, Tablets and Smartphones Regularly**
- **Step III - Keep Operating Systems and Applications Updated**
- **Step IV - Install and Maintain a Third-Party Internet Security Suite**
- **Step V - Limit Access to Personal Information (Location, Browsing History, etc.)**
- **Step VI - Encrypt Your Computer, Tablet, Smartphone, and Important Files**

These six practices, when properly applied, will significantly increase your protective posture. The first four practices focus on cyber security and the last two focus on privacy. The good news is that many of these actions are "set it and forget it!" Once it is set up, everything will be performed without you having to set time aside to work on it regularly. This is important because there is a tradeoff when it comes to security and convenience. A smartphone with no passcode is very easy to use, but it is less secure. A website that requires you to enter a username, password, and multi-factor code to enter is less convenient to log into but is more secure.

Use Unique Passphrases and Multi-Factor Authentication for Your Online Accounts

STEP I

Use Unique Passphrases and Multi-Factor Authentication for your Online Accounts

Earlier, we discussed the comparison of your email address and password being the "keys" to your online accounts. You would never use the same key for your house, car, and office. The same goes for your email address and password for your various online accounts. No matter how long or complicated your password may be, if you use the same password on all of your accounts, all of your accounts may be compromised if there is a single breach.

In 2019, my email address and password were stolen in an attack on the popular social-planning website. If I had used the same email address and passwords on all of my accounts, the criminal hackers would have been able to log into my banking, travel, and other accounts with ease. The bad actors use applications that try your same email address and password on hundreds of sites to see what else they can exploit using the information they stole. It was not my fault that my email address and password were stolen, but it would be my fault if the criminal hackers used those credentials to log into my other accounts. It can't be overstated how important it is to use unique passwords for all of your online accounts.

I know what some of you are thinking —"I have dozens of accounts! How do you expect me to remember dozens of unique passwords?!?!?" I would not ask you to use unique passwords without providing you with a technique on how to do it. We start by losing the term "password" and start using the term **"Two-Part Passphrase."** We create Two-Part Passphrases in two simple steps:

STEP 1: – Create the Base of the Two-Part Passphrases

A passphrase base uses the first letter of each word in a sentence from your favorite song, poem or other document instead of the variation of a standard word. For example, could you remember this as the first part of your two-part passphrase : Ip@ttF0tUS0@ Don't think you could remember this? Are you sure? Do you know the first line from the American Pledge of Allegiance? - "I pledge allegiance...to the flag...of the United States of America." I merely took the first letter from that sentence, switched a couple of the vowels for special characters and voila! Go ahead, try it with your favorite song or poem:

Ex: "Rolling in the Deep" by Adele

"We could have had it all. Rolling in the deep."

Passphrase: Wchh!@R!td

Ex: "Stopping by Woods On a Snowy Evening" by Robert Frost
"But I have promises to keep. And miles to go before I sleep."

Passphrase: B!hp2k@m2gb!$

With a few substitutions (! instead of the letter "i", the number 2 instead of the word "to", etc.), you have a complex base for your two-part passphrase.

STEP 2: – Connect the Website You Use to the Passphrase Base

In the 21st century, the average person has logins for dozens of websites. In order to use unique passphrases for each website, you merely need to add a simple suffix to the first part of the passphrase created in Step 1. Here are some examples:

Passphrase Base for Bank of America: Ip@ttF0tUS0@
Website Identifier for Bank of America: BOA
Full Passphrase for Bank of America: Ip@ttF0tUS0@BOA

Passphrase Base for Amazon: Ip@ttF0tUS0@
Website Identifier for Amazon: AMZ
Full Passphrase for Amazon: Ip@ttF0tUS0@AMZ

The passphrases for both websites are unique. If the Bank of America passphrase is ever compromised, it cannot be used to log into Amazon. This same passphrase technique can be used for all of your online accounts:

Google: Ip@ttF0tUS0@GOO
YouTube: Ip@ttF0tUS0@YOU
Facebook: Ip@ttF0tUS0@FB
Twitter: Ip@ttF0tUS0@TWI
Wikipedia: Ip@ttF0tUS0@WIK
Instagram: Ip@ttF0tUS0@INS
Yahoo: Ip@ttF0tUS0@YAH

You don't have to use the first three letters of a website as your suffix. You could use one letter, but your Amazon and Ameritrade account passphrases would be the same. Whatever suffix you choose, be sure that you remain consistent so that you don't forget your passphrase. For example:

Twitter: Ip@ttF0tUS0@twi
Last three lower case letters in the name of site

Twitter: Ip@ttF0tUS0@STW
S for "Social Media" and the letters of the site

Twitter: Ip@ttF0tUS0@4TWI
The number 4 instead of "for" and the site

If you are stubborn and do not want to give up the password you have been using for a while, there is still hope. Take your old password and give it a strong, unique suffix. For example, if your current password is "Password1", you can turn it into a unique passphrase by adding "@B0A!". The "@"sign and exclamation point in addition to the site reference makes the passphrase unique and much more secure. The same for all of the other website passwords:

Google: Password1@G00!
YouTube: Password1@YOU!
Facebook: Password1@FAC!
Twitter: Password1@TWI!
Wikipedia: Password1@WIK!
Instagram: Password1@INS!
Yahoo: Password1@YAH!

Whether you use the passphrase technique above or develop your own system for remembering complex passphrases, the goal is to make the passphrases for your accounts unique and complex. In the event of a major hack, the last things that you want to do is scramble to change the passwords for Amazon, eBay, PayPal, Google, Walmart, Uber, Etsy, Ameritrade, Microsoft, Home Depot, Facebook, Target, LinkedIn, Chipotle, Apple, Best Buy, Lowes, Wayfair, Spotify, Burger King, Ring, Costco, Macy's, Twitter, Kohls, Trip Advisor, Instagram, CVS, Gap, Walgreens, Bank of America, Evite, Subway, Outback, AirBnB, Panera Bread, AMC, Overstock, Chick-fil-A, LG, Netflix, DoorDash, Sam's Club, Audible, McDonald's, Lyft, Chewy, Ticketmaster, Wendy's, Nike, Experian, Samsung, Poshmark, Dominos, Weebly, QVC, Robinhood, Bed Bath & Beyond, Chase, Total Wine, Ikea, Booking, Shopify, Kroger, Expedia, Pizza Hut, and whatever email systems you are using.

That's right, you probably have more online accounts than you immediately remember. Some passwords may have been created years ago and have not been used for some time. Some were created for free delivery or a discount on purchases. Other accounts may be used often and have stored credit card information in them. If all of your online accounts have the same password, you are in for a very long evening trying to change them all if one is compromised. Hopefully, your passwords can be changed before a criminal hacker logs into the accounts and causes problems for you and your credit card companies. That would lead to many more hours, days or even weeks of phone calls and email messages trying to undo the damage that could have been avoided by using complex, unique passphrases.

Even complex, unique passphrases are not enough to secure your most important online actions. Multi-factor authentication (MFA), also known as Two-Factor Authentication (2FA) is a code that you must enter after your username and password in order to gain access to an account. MFA/2FA provides a critical and much-needed layer of protection to important online accounts. When you login to an account, you need a "factor", which is your password (or now hopefully a passphrase) to gain access. By adding another factor, bad actors cannot log into your account if they know or steal your password. This additional factor comes in many forms:

- Something You Know: Secondary Password or PIN
- Something You Have: Digital Certificate, MFA token, dongle or smartphone app
- Something You Are: Biometrics (Fingerprints, Facial Recognition)

There are many MFA options currently offered by consumer websites. Physical MFA devices are typically used by businesses, not normal consumers. There is an administrative burden associated with tracking MFA devices and quickly replacing them when they are lost or forgotten. Having a third-party MFA code app on your smartphone is the safest and easiest way to receive your MFA code. MFA apps are not designed to be viewed from multiple devices at the same time. For this reason, bad actors will not have access to your code if you have your smartphone. The likelihood that you are going to forget your smartphone at home is much lower than forgetting your physical MFA device. The code in the smartphone app typically changes every 60 seconds, so waiting until the last second to send the code provides a degree of protection against the code being intercepted. Many MFA code apps provide the option to select "Approve / Yes" or "Disapprove / No" after a password has been entered to log into an account. Selecting "yes" or "no" instead of entering a code makes the MFA process much easier and faster.

Receiving an MFA code via text/SMS is quick and convenient, but is not considered as secure as an MFA app. When an MFA code is delivered by email, the email can be viewed by anyone with access to your email account. This is not usually a problem unless your email account has already been compromised, and you are unknowingly sending the MFA code to yourself and the bad actors at the same time. If your MFA code is currently being delivered via email, consider changing your settings to MFA code by app if possible.

When you have MFA enabled, even if there is a major business hack and the bad actors have your email address and password, they cannot access your account. Without that second factor, the bad actors will just move onto the next account on their list to plunder. In 2019, Microsoft reported that "multi-factor authentication can prevent 99.9 percent of attacks on your accounts." If that's not a compelling reason to enable MFA, I don't know what is. While using the MFA process may be bothersome to some, spending 15-20 seconds to supply an MFA when logging into your account is worth the 99.9% security assurance in return. When your account is not protected by MFA, if it is compromised and funds are stolen, you will spend much more than 15-20 seconds on the phone with your financial institutions trying to get any stolen funds returned.

Applying unique passphrases and MFA to your online accounts is not hard and it's worth the effort. Remember that the goal is to make yourself a harder target. We want the bad actors to hit as many speed bumps on the way to your information as possible. Using strong, unique passwords and multifactor authentication is the first and most impactful step to securing your information.

STEP II

Backup Your Computers, Smartphones and Tablets Regularly

STEP II

Back Up Your Computers, Smartphones and Tablets Regularly

When it comes to computers, there are few things more precious to an information technology professional than a good backup. One of the first questions asked when a computer is damaged, or a smartphone is lost is "Do we have a backup?" After a computing device is damaged, stolen, or criminally hacked, getting "back to normal" is everyone's goal. There is no better way to reach that goal quickly than to have a good backup. Backing up data is important, but backing up your data, apps, and operating system at the same time (aka Full Backup) is better. Ideally, you want to back up your data, apps, and operating system all at once, using one process. Fortunately, our modern desktop and laptop operating systems make the backup process pretty easy. You can back up your computers, tablets and smartphones locally (to a computer or external hard drive) or to the cloud. The same goes for your data. You just have to set it up. Below are a few techniques to back up your computers, tablets and smartphones. These techniques may change as operating systems are updated, so always ensure that you have checked online for the latest back up procedures for your devices.

Performing a Local Backup - Windows 10 Computer:

- Purchase a new encrypted external USB hard drive to be used exclusively for full backups.
- Plug the external hard drive into the computer and let Windows 10 recognize it.
- Rename the hard drive so that you know what it is used for, but do not make it obvious to someone else that may come across the drive.
- Open "Settings" from the main Windows menu.
- Click on "Update & Security", then backup.
- In the section "Looking for an older backup?", click the "Go to Backup and Restore (Windows 7)".
- ***PAUSE*** – *You may be thinking "Why in the heck am I performing a backup from an operating system that is no longer supported?" The answer is – it works really well when backing up the entire computer. Now back to the backup. . .*
- Click "Create a system image" on the left. A system image is another name for a complete backup of a computer.
- Click "On Hard Disk", then select the external hard drive that you set up earlier, then click "Next"
- You will then have the option to select the hard drives to Backup. Select all drives except for the external hard drive you are backing up to.
- Select "Next", then "Start Backup".
- When prompted to create a system repair disk, select "No". If you ever need to restore from a backup, there are several ways to complete the task without the repair disk.

Performing a Local Backup – Apple Mac Computer:

- Purchase a new external USB hard drive to be used exclusively for full backups.

Performing a Local Backup – Apple Mac Computer (cont.)

- Plug the external hard drive into the computer and let macOS recognize it.
- Rename the hard drive so that you know what it used for, but not make it obvious to someone else that may come across the drive.
- Under "Preferences," click the "Time Machine" icon.
- Click the "Select Backup Disk" box to select the new external hard drive that you just plugged in and renamed.
- Check the box "Encrypt Backups" to make sure the backups cannot be compromised, then click the "Use Disk" box.
- You may be prompted to format the disk, especially if this is a new disk. This disk should only be used for "Time Machine" backups, so formatting is fine.

Performing a Local Backup – Android Tablet or Smartphone

You can Backup files and folders on an Android tablet or smartphone using the Android File Transfer app from the official Android website:

- After installing the Android File Transfer app, plug the Android tablet or smartphone into the computer via USB cable.
- Start the Android File Transfer app.
- Select the files and folders that you want to save to your computer and click "Copy" to move the files to your computer.

Backup an Android Tablet or Smartphone to the Cloud:

- Open the "Settings" app, then tap on "System", then "Backup".
- Make sure that the "Backup to Google Drive" toggle is in the "On" position.
- Tap "Backup Now".

Performing a Local Backup – Apple Tablet or Smartphone:

- Make sure that you have the latest version of iTunes installed on your computer.
- Open iTunes, then plug in your Apple tablet or smartphone.
- If your device prompts you to "Trust This Computer" or enter your passcode, please do so.
- Once the device appears on the left side of the iTunes screen, click on it.
- Under the "General" tab, locate the "Backup" area.
- Select "Backup all of the data" option and check the "Encrypt Local Backup" box.
- Click "Backup Now".

Backup an Apple Tablet or Smartphone to the Cloud:

- Open the "Settings" app, then tap on your name / icon, then "iCloud".
- Tap "iCloud Backup", then tap "Backup Now".

Backup an Google Chromebook:

For Chromebook users, some data is backed up automatically on the Google cloud. This data includes browsing history and bookmarks, web browser extensions and apps, device theme and wallpaper, web browser settings, web browser autofill passwords, payment methods, and addresses, Google Play Android apps (but not app data). To backup locally saved files:

- Open the "Files" app.
- In each of the folders (ex. Downloads, Play Files", Edits), select all of the files.
- Right-click on the selected files and click "Copy".
- On the left, click on the "Google Drive" icon.
- Click on the folder you want to copy your local files to.
- Right-click on the folder then click "Paste".

There are several third-party applications that make backing up your computer, tablet and smartphone easier. I will not recommend one backup application over another, and I will not recommend using a backup app over the methods covered in this chapter. The only thing that I recommend is that you choose a process to back up your computers, tablets and smartphones and stick with it. Back up your computers regularly. If you are backing up to an external hard drive, schedule it on the weekends. When you are backing up to the cloud, backup every 5 days, depending on how often your files change. If the option is available, turn on the *automatic backup* feature so your backups will occur on a regular schedule.

Choosing to backup your devices to a local drive or the cloud is a personal decision. If you choose the cloud, you are putting your personal information in the hands of a large corporation, hoping that they do not misuse it. If you back up to an external hard drive, you trust that the drive does not fail. Speaking of failing external hard drives, if you are backing up your external hard drive, consider keeping the drive in your home fireproof safe. Backing up to an external hard drive is simple, but if an unfortunate event like a home burglary or fire occurs, you will lose your backup along with your computer. Again, it does not matter what method you choose, as long as you choose an action and regularly back up your devices.

STEP III

Keep Operating Systems and Applications Updated

STEP III

Keep Operating Systems and Applications Updated

In 2003, Microsoft founder Bill Gates said, "You don't need perfect code to avoid security problems." The statement is true for a couple of reasons. One reason is that there is no such thing as perfect code. Software engineering is an amazing discipline and there are many incredibly talented coders out there, but no matter how smart a coder is, there is someone equally as smart that can find a flaw in the code that can be exploited to compromise your device. One of Bill Gates' solutions to mitigate the impact of imperfect code is to "keep the software up to date." Updating software patches the holes that are discovered so that the flaws cannot be exploited by bad actors. It is a good practice to perform data and system backups. In the rare occurrence that an update fails or causes a problem on your device, you can always restore your system from the last good backup.

There are three categories of software that require updating: Applications (Apps), Operating Systems, and Firmware:

- Apps – We all know apps. We love apps. From messaging and social media apps, to those gaming apps that we spend hours on with friends, apps are the main reason we cannot live without our smartphones. There are close to five million apps available for smartphones. Add to that number the hundreds of thousands of apps written for computers and you have a tremendous amount of code out there for bad actors to choose from.

- Operating Systems – An operating system (OS) is the software that allows you to run the apps. Fortunately, there are far fewer operating systems to choose from. The two primary computer operating systems we will cover in this book are Microsoft Windows (WinOS) and Apple Mac Operating System (macOS). The two primary smartphone operating systems we will cover are Apple's iPhone Operating System (iOS), Google Android (AOS, but most people just say Android), and Google ChromeOS, used in ChromeBooks.

- Firmware - Firmware is the software that runs a device's hardware. The chips on the motherboard, the memory, the screen, the hard drive – all of the components that make a computing device run. For computers, updating the firmware is not a common occurrence. For home routers and Internet of Things (IoT) devices like Wi-Fi cameras, firmware updates occur more frequently (more on IoT later).

Some of you may think that all of this updating sounds like a lot of work. The good news is that some updates can be done automatically. Let's start with the easy ones:

- **Automatically Update the Windows 10 Operating System**

  - IMPORTANT: Always completely back up your system before updating the operating system. Additionally, for Windows computers, create a new Restore Point. If you cannot back up to the cloud, back up to an external hard drive.

- Select the Start button, then select Settings > Update & security > Windows Update.

- Select Advanced Options, and then under Choose how updates are installed, select Automatic (recommended).

  NOTE: As of January 2021, if you are using Windows 8, Windows 7 or earlier, mainstream support for the operating system has ended. Extended support for Windows 8.1, which includes "Critical" and/or "Important" security updates, ends in 2023. Updating to Windows 10 to receive all available updates if the recommended course of action. Any device running an unsupported operating system runs an extreme risk of compromise when operating on a network, including the Internet.

- **Automatically Update the Windows 10 Apps**

  - Select the "Start" screen, then select "Microsoft Store"

  - In the upper right area of the store, select the three dots for the "Account" menu, then select "Settings".

  - Under "App Updates", switch the "Update Apps Automatically" to the on position.

    NOTE: If you installed apps without going through the Microsoft Store, you will have to update the apps manually. This is usually done by opening the app, clicking the menu buttons on the top to look for an "Update" button (usually under the 'Help' menu).

  - <u>NEVER</u> update apps from a pop-up message on the screen. Some of the messages that appear when you have a browser open may be malicious. If you receive a pop-up message telling you to update your app, close the pop-up message and perform a manual update.

- **Automatically Update the Apple macOS Operating System and Apps**

  - IMPORTANT: Always completely backup your system before updating the operating system. If you cannot backup to the cloud, backup to an external hard drive.
  - On your Mac, choose Apple menu > System Preferences > Software Update.
  - Select "Automatically keep my Mac up to date" box.
  - Click the "Advanced," button:
  - Check all of the update boxes presented to automatically:

    - Check for updates
    - Download new updates when available
    - Install macOS updates
    - Install app updates from the App Store
    - Install system data files and security updates

  - Click OK

    NOTE: As of January 2021, if you are using Apple Mac operating system version 10.13 (High Sierra) or earlier, support for the operating system has ended. Updating to macOS 10.14 (Mojave) or higher to receive all available updates is the recommended course of action. Any device running an unsupported operating system runs an extreme risk of compromise when operating on a network, including the Internet.

- **Automatically Update the Apps on an Android Device**

  - Open the "Google Play Store" app.

- In the upper-left area of the screen, tap on the three lines, then tap "Settings".
- Select the "General" tab then select the "Auto Update Apps" button.

- **Update the Android Operating System on Smartphones and Tablets**

  - **IMPORTANT:** Always completely back up your device before updating the operating system. You can typically back up a mobile device to the Google cloud.

  - You should receive an update message on your Android device when an update is available. Since Android device operating systems are sometimes customized by the device manufacturer, the automatic update options may vary. If you do not receive automatic update messages, perform manual updates regularly:

    - Open the Android "Settings" app.
    - Tap on "System", then "Advanced", then "System update".
    - Follow any instructions that appear on the screen to complete the update.
    - **NOTE:** Security updates and Google Play updates may not apply during a system update. To apply those updates, complete the following steps:
    - Click on the Android "Settings" app.
    - Tap "Security", then tap "Security Update".
    - When that process completes, tap "Google Play system update".

    NOTE: As of January 2021, if you are using a device with an Android operating system version 8.0 (Oreo) or earlier, support for the operating system has ended. Update all Android devices to OS version 8.1 or higher to receive all available updates. Any device running an unsupported operating system runs an extreme risk of compromise when operating on a network, including the Internet.

- **Automatically Update the Apple iOS and iPadOS Operating System**

  - **IMPORTANT**: Always completely back up your device before updating the operating system. You can typically update Apple devices to iCloud.
  - Open the "Settings" app.
  - Tap "General", "Software Update", then "Automatic Updates".
  - Turn on both the download updates and install update buttons.

- **Automatically Update Apps for Apple iOS and iPadOS**

  - Open the "Settings" app.
  - Scroll down and tap "App Store".
  - Switch the "App Updates" switch to "On".

- **Manually Update Apps for Apple iOS and iPadOS**

  - Open the "App Store" app.
  - Tap the account icon in the upper-right area of the screen. It may be your initials or your profile picture if you set one up.
  - Swipe down from anywhere on the screen to update the list of available app updates.

  - Tap the words "Update All" to start the update process.

- Tap "Done" in the upper right area of the screen when done.

- **Automatically Update Google ChromeOS for Chromebooks**

  - **IMPORTANT:** Always completely back up your device before updating the operating system. You can typically back up a ChromeBook to your Google Drive.
  - Click on the "Settings" tray in the lower-right area of the screen.
  - Click on the gear-looking icon.
  - Click "About Chrome OS" then click "Check for updates".
  - If updates are available, wait until the process the update finishes downloading, click "Restart".

It is critically important to update your IoT devices regularly. An IoT device is a non-traditional computing device (not a desktop, laptop, or smartphone) that connects to a network and transmits data. IoT devices include (but are not limited to) smart televisions, virtual assistants, smart watches, home thermostats, smart doorbells, Wi-Fi connected security cameras, smart door locks, smart light switches and light bulbs, wireless trackers, and Wi-Fi enabled cameras. Traditional appliances that have network connections (coffee makers, refrigerators, etc.) are also categorized as IoT devices. Unlike most computers and smartphones, IoT devices do not always notify you when there is a system or security update. If your IoT device does not automatically update itself, you should manually check for updates regularly. Once a month is a good interval, but with new IoT devices appearing all the time, it's better to do the pre-purchase research and buy IoT devices that update automatically.

Whether it is an operating system, an app or an IoT device, updating devices is a critically important exercise. Just like changing the oil in a car, it's something that you should do regularly to avoid problems. Unlike changing your oil, you don't have to get dirty, and it does not require a professional. All you need is a little time, a little patience, and a little knowledge. Hopefully this chapter provides the knowledge you need to keep your devices updated.

STEP IV

**Install and Maintain a
Third-Party Internet
Security Suite**

STEP IV

Install and Maintain a Third-Party Internet Security Suite

Now that we are all patched and up to date, that means that we are safe, right? Unfortunately, no. We have only covered two of the six cans in our six pack. This third can be the most controversial because it challenges a lot of established beliefs surrounding the built-in security of operating systems. I am not challenging statements from Microsoft, Apple or Google about the effectiveness of their built-in security. I am simply promoting the idea that an additional layer of security for devices that contain our important information is a good thing and is easy to implement. There are at least a dozen reputable third-party Internet security suite companies to choose from. These companies are focused on securing digital devices. They do not focus on making word processing or spreadsheet software. Their revenue is based on how well they protect your devices. I have used a dozen different internet security suites in my lifetime. Some were good, some were very good, and some were horrible. Instead of focusing on which third-party security company to go with, I want to focus on the features that should be included in your selected product.

- Malware Protection - Protects your device from malware such as viruses, worms, spyware, and adware. This feature typically uses patterns/signatures of known malware to identify malicious files and processes.

- <u>Two-Way Firewall</u> – A firewall identifies the network traffic passing through a computing device and blocks traffic that is not permitted or the appears malicious. Most firewalls only examine incoming traffic, or traffic traveling into the computer from the network or Internet. A two-way firewall is especially useful in identifying and blocking malware or applications that create new or dangerous connections out to the Internet.

- <u>Ransomware Protection</u> – Ransomware is malware that infects your computer, encrypts all of your files, then displays a message demanding a ransom to be paid to gain access to your files. Ransomware protection detects when malicious file encryption is taking place, stops the encryption, then deletes the malware that started the encryption. Given that ransomware costs individuals and businesses tens of billions each year, this feature is one of the more important components of any security suite.

- <u>Host-Based Intrusion Detection / Prevention</u> – Host-based intrusion detection systems (HIDS) and host-based intrusion prevention systems (HIPS) monitor network traffic traveling to and from the computer for malicious activity. HIDS/HIPS can detect new threats that malware protection modules may not have signatures for.

- <u>Behavior Anomaly Detection</u> – This component detects patterns of behavior that do not conform to a normal or expected behavior and either alerts on or stops the behavior. For example, if a bad actor installs program on your system with the same "paint.exe" (the default Windows drawing application), and that program tries to go out on the Internet, that unexpected behavior would be stopped.

- Secure Browser or Browser Plug-In / Extension – Some security suites offer a secure browser plug-in (or extension, depending on the browser) for all of your installed browsers. The plug-in / extension will block malicious URLs (websites) and also mark search engine results safe, dangerous or unknown. These plug-ins are one of the few browser plug-ins that I recommend. A secure browser is an option that is mainly for smartphones and tablets. Instead of modifying the browser app (which is not permitted in some cases), you are provided with a secure browser that has all the features of the browser plug-in/extension.

- URL Filtering – URL filtering works like a secure browser plug-in / extension, but does not require you to add anything on to the browser. The feature will look at all connections to URLs (websites) and block anything that is deemed malicious. The URL filter can also be configured to block entire classes of URLs, like gambling, pornography and illegal narcotics.

- Email Filter – This feature blocks spam, phishing, spoofing, zero-day attacks, and malware on incoming email. Email threats, especially phishing, are on the rise. This feature should be mandatory for any third-party security suite purchased.

- Webcam & Microphone In-Use Notification – Bad actors can install malware that controls the webcam and microphone on computers to spy on people. Webcam and microphone in-use notification does just what the name implies- displays a warning message or icon when either the microphone or webcam is in use. This icon will be visible when participating in video conferences (Zoom, Teams, etc.). If the warning message or icon is visible at any other time, your computer is probably compromised.

- Parental Controls - Parental controls are settings that allow an adult to limit activities on a computer, smartphone or tablet. These activities include limiting access to specific websites, preventing access to entire categories of websites (adult, gambling, etc.), preventing unauthorized purchases and limiting time on the devices.

- Password Manager – A password manager securely stores your passwords and adds them to your login pages as requested. Unlike saving passwords in a browser (a big no-no), a password manager can be used on multiple computers and mobile devices.

- Additional Features – Depending on the company, Internet security suites offer additional features such as cloud backup, virtual private networking (VPN), privacy monitoring, credit monitoring, and breach notifications. More features do not necessarily mean that the product is better. When it comes to endpoint security products, performance is more important than features. Be sure to compare products online and read reviews before purchasing.

One of the biggest complaints about third party Internet security suites is the cost. Fortunately, costs have gone down in the sense that you can now install the suite on five to ten family computers, depending on the vendor. If you don't have five to ten computers, share your license with your parents and siblings (technically, still a family member's computer). The goal is to make everyone safer than before. The cost of an effective third-party internet security suite is less than what one would pay for a professional to work on an infected computer for an hour.

When dealing with an infected computer, I have spent no less than three hours clearing out infections on the computers of family members. Because I love my family, I work on their infected computers in exchange for a good home-cooked meal. Depending on where you live, a full PC cleanup could cost several hundred dollars. The ironic part of a cleanup is that you end up purchasing an Internet security suite anyway. This is a textbook case of an ounce of prevention being worth a pound of cure – in this case – an ounce of prevention saves hours of cleanup.

STEP V

Limit Access to Personal Information

STEP V

Limit Access to Personal Information

The Internet thrives on the exchange of personal information. The question is - how much personal information is too much personal information? Limiting access to your personal information is a shared responsibility. You have a responsibility to understand the value of the information you share. The companies you share your information with have a responsibility to protect that information. As the world learned from the Equifax hack of 2017, even the big, reputable, well-protected companies can suffer a data breach. That means that each one of us has a greater responsibility to safeguard our personal information. As stated earlier in the book, information is the lifeblood of the Internet. Your information equals money. The "free services" like social media and chat services will be made available to you as long as you supply information. Remember:

- You can give a little information.
- You can give a lot of information.
- You can give accurate information.
- You can give completely made-up information

No matter what information you give, you can use the service. It is completely up to you. While I am not encouraging you to provide false information and deceive people online, I am encouraging you to limit the information you provide.

Personal information can be divided into two categories – Private and Sensitive:

- Private information is any piece of data that can be used to identify you with some degree of accuracy. This information includes (but is not limited to):

    - Name (first, middle, last)
    - Home address
    - Email address
    - An identification card number
    - Location data
    - Internet Protocol (IP) address
    - Advertising identifier of your phone

- Sensitive personal information is data that requires extra security. This information includes (but is not limited to):

    - Health conditions
    - Credit card number
    - Social Security number
    - Race – Ethnicity - Gender
    - Political affiliation or opinions
    - Religious or philosophical beliefs
    - Group membership (unions, nonpartisan organizations, partisan organizations)
    - Genetic data
    - Biometric data

Private and sensitive information both require thought and discernment before sharing. Sensitive information should be shared only when absolutely required. The more information you share, the more precise and target the online and email advertisements will be.

While that sounds good to some people, do you really want a bunch of advertisers knowing you that well? Knowing what you like to eat, what candidate you will vote for, where you like to get your coffee–knowing WHEN you are going to get your next cup of coffee?!?!?! That's right, there is a dangerous side to all of that information you share. With enough information, the companies and advertisers can predict what you are going to do. That's why it is critical to preserve as much of your personal information as possible when using online services.

Here are a few tips to help preserve some of your privacy:

Check Your Operating System Privacy Settings

Each computer, tablet, and smartphone operating systems come with a set of privacy settings. There are literally dozens and dozens of security settings for each operating system (location restrictions, camera and microphone restrictions, etc.), far too many to document in this book. The starting points for each operating system are:

Windows 10:

- Launch "Settings", then click "Privacy".
- Launch "Settings", then click "Privacy".
- Under "Windows Permissions", start with "General" and disable the settings that you are not comfortable with.
- Continue through different sections under both "Windows Permissions" and "App Permissions,

disabling each setting that you are not comfortable with.

- If you do not know how the settings may impact the performance of your computer, go through the "Have a Question" section in each privacy category.

Apple macOS

- Click on the Apple icon in the upper left corner, then "System Preferences".
- Click the "Security and Privacy" icon, then click on the "Privacy" tab.
- Starting with "Location Services", go through all the privacy options and disable any settings that you are not comfortable with. If you do not know how the settings may impact the performance of your computer, please research the settings online before changing them.

ChromeOS

- Move the cursor down to the lower-right of the screen and click the oval containing the time and battery information.
- Click on gear icon to bring up the "Settings" menu.
- Click on "Advanced Settings" then click "Privacy and Security".
- Go through all the privacy options and disable any settings that you are not comfortable with. If you do not know how the settings may affect the performance of your computer, please

research the settings online before changing them.

Android Tablets and Smartphones

- **NOTE:** Due to the large number of Android device manufacturers, the operating system settings may vary.
- Open the "Settings" app then tap "Privacy".
- Go through all the privacy options and disable any settings that you are not comfortable with. If you do not know how the settings may impact the performance of your computer, please research the settings online before changing them.

Apple iOS and ipadOS

- Open the "Settings" app then tap "Privacy".
- Go through all the privacy options and disable any settings that you are not comfortable with. If you do not know how the settings may impact the performance of your computer, please research the settings online before changing them.

Check Your App Privacy Settings

- Even though you may disable some of the privacy settings on your device's operating system, there are additional settings in your apps that should be checked. Going through the privacy settings for the hundreds of thousands of apps available is impossible, but the privacy settings to look for include:

- Location Settings
- History and Cookies
- Ad Accuracy
- Profile Information Sharing
- Public and Private Postings
- Your Tags and Who Can Tag You
- Activity Log

Use Multiple Email Addresses for Apps and Online Services

- Many people have a personal email address and a work/ school email address, but given the number of apps we use, you need a lot more email addresses to protect your privacy. To keep your personal life personal, create special purpose email accounts. Since most email apps for computers and mobile devices allow you to view all new messages in a combined fashion, you do not need to log into separate accounts to manage your new messages. Here are a few examples of email accounts to create:

Personal / Family Email Address

- This is the email address that you use with close family members and important official contacts (government sites, insurance companies, doctor's offices, banking, etc.). Whether you are applying for loans or submitting your tax information online, it's important that you have an email account that is free from the clutter of advertisements.

Social Media Email Address

- Keeping your social media email address separate from your personal email address is critical to preserving your privacy. If you use social media and want to keep down on the number of email addresses, this should be one of the two you use.

Travel Email Address

- If you use ride sharing and other airline, hotel, and other travel apps, they come with a lot of advertising email messages. Sending those messages to a separate email address keeps your important messages from being lost in travel advertisement clutter.

Food Email Address

- Just like travel email advertisements, food email advertisements can overwhelm an inbox (especially if you love fast food apps). You don't use just one email address and have to send dozens of these messages to spam–especially for BOGO specials–so send them to their own email address.

Contest Email Address

- If you like to enter contests online, having a separate contest email address is a must. The amount of spam you receive after entering a contest is staggering. You don't want to give a contest your primary email address and have to deal with years of spam, especially when you don't win the contest.

NOTE: You don't have to use radically different email addresses. For example:

- Personal: john.doe@emailaddress.com
- Social Media: john.s.doe@emailaddress.com
- Travel: john.t.doe@emailaddress.com
- Food: john.f.doe@emailaddress.com
- Contest: john.c.doe@emailaddress.com

One important benefit of using different email addresses is quickly identifying phishing messages. If you receive a message that purports to come from your bank, but comes in on your contest email account, you instantly know that it is a fake email.

<u>Use a VPN App (Especially when using public Wi-Fi)</u>

- When communicating over the Internet, any information not encrypted in a HTTPS browser session may be readable as it passes through the network equipment that runs the Internet. Virtual Private Networking (VPN) creates an encrypted line of communication (aka VPN Tunnel) between your device and your VPN provider or target VPN endpoint. This includes the wireless access points we connect to for Wi-Fi access. Many corporations use VPN, so the communications between their mobile employee computer and the company are encrypted and safe from snooping. The VPN app protects your information similarly, but only protects your information between your device and your VPN provider. While not end-to-end protection like a corporate VPN, there is enough protection that you can safely use public Wi-Fi. Having a VPN app is great if you frequently travel and use the Wi-Fi in coffee shops and hotels. It is better to go with a paid VPN service as they are faster, more reliable, and have more states and countries to choose from as you travel. While free VPN apps are available, remember what I stated about "free" Internet services in an earlier chapter.

Browse in Private Mode

- All the most popular Internet browsers offer a form of "Private Mode" browsing. Generally speaking, a web browser retains until you manually delete it. Even if you close the browser and restart the computer, that information is retained in the browser. Private Mode browsing only keeps that information if the browser is in use. Close the browser and that information will be erased. There are some websites that prevent you from viewing their content while in Private Mode. That's a hint and a half, telling you they would like access to the information saved in your browser. If you encounter a site like that, manually clear all your browsing data before leaving "Private Mode." If you really want to browse privately, you may want to use browsers and search engines dedicated to maximizing privacy. There are several good options available. Do your research and find the browser and search engine that you are most comfortable using.

Use Messaging and Conferencing Apps with End-to-End Encryption

- The COVID-19 Pandemic that challenged the world in the year 2020 ushered in a new era of Internet-based communications. Not only did messaging app use increase, but the use of video conference apps also exploded. When using messaging and video conferencing apps, it is important that the apps feature end-to-end encryption. In other words, if you do not want your conversations to be intercepted by any of the networking devices that make up the Internet, avoid using any communication apps that do not feature end-to-end encryption. Keep your private conversations private.

As stated earlier, limiting access to your personal information is a shared responsibility, but most of the responsibility is on you. You must take the initiative to implement the proper settings on your browsers and apps, not use the same email address for all your apps and accounts, and secure your communications using VPN and end-to-end encrypted apps. The good news about making these changes to better your privacy is that once you make the changes, you do not have to keep changing them. Set it and forget it – unless you want to become even more secure and tighten them up a little more.

STEP VI

**Encrypt Your
Computer, Tablet,
Smartphone,
and Important Files**

STEP VI

Encrypt Your Computer, Tablet, Smartphone, and Important Files

When a computer, tablet or smartphone is lost or stolen, there can be feelings of disappointment and anxiety. Disappointment that you no longer have your valuable piece of electronics and it will cost a fair amount of money to replace. Knowing that a device with your personal information may be in the hands of a bad actor would make anyone anxious. If your device has one of the "Find My Device" features enabled, you may be able to track your device down. Unfortunately, a bad actor might be trying to access the data on your computer, tablet or smartphone. The best way to prevent personal data from being extracted from lost or stolen devices is to encrypt the hard drives of the devices. In the past, encrypting a computer's hard drive was unpopular because it impacted the computer's performance. Modern encryption practices minimize the impact on computer performance and should be considered mandatory for people that use laptops and travel often, even if it is just to work or school.

Microsoft Windows Encryption

- Windows 10 Pro:

- Click on the Windows Start Menu button, then click "Control Panel".
- Click on "System and Security" then click "BitLocker Drive Encryption".
- Click "Turn on "BitLocker".
- Save your Recovery Key in a safe place.
- Select "Encrypt the entire hard drive".
- Check the "Run BitLocker System Check" box then click "Continue".
- Restart your computer to start the drive encryption process.

- <u>Windows 10 Home:</u>

  - Open "Settings".
  - Click on "Update & Security".
  - Click on "Device Encryption". If you do not see "Device encryption" your computer may not support drive encryption. Contact Microsoft directly.
  - Click "Turn On".

<u>Apple macOS Encryption</u>

- On your Mac, choose Apple menu > System Preferences > Security & Privacy.
- Click on the "FileVault tab.
- Click "Turn on FileVault . . ."
- When prompted, enter your username and password to approve the encryption process.
- Save your Recovery Key in a safe place in case you ever need it.

<u>Google Chromebook</u>

- Chromebook users are in luck. As soon as you sign into a Chromebook, the device creates a private, encrypted area for use. Even if the Chromebook's hard drive is removed, no one can access the data on it.

Encrypting your mobile devices is just as important as encrypting your computer, because these devices are lost and stolen more often.

Android Tablets and Smartphones

- **NOTE:** Depending on the model, some Android tablets and smartphones arrive with encryption enabled. Check with your device manufacturers.
- **NOTE:** Due to the large number of Android device manufacturers, the device encryption settings may vary.
- Make sure that device has a passcode enabled. Not only is this a sound security practice, but it is also a requirement for encryption.
- Open the "Settings" app, then tap "Security" and "Encrypt Device".
  - o If prompted for encryption location, choose storage encryption.
- Follow the instructions to complete the encryption process.

Apple Tablets and Smartphones

- Fortunately for Apple tablets and smartphones, encryption is enabled by default. As long as the device has a passcode enabled, the device is safe.

Full disk encryption is a great way to protect your information if your computer is lost or stolen, but what if you share a computer and want to protect sensitive files? An encrypted folder is just like any folder, but the folder has its own encryption settings, separate from the full-disk encryption. You must enter a password to access the contents of the folder, so if a bad actor happens to get a copy of the folder, they will not have access to the data. This is a great way to store very sensitive files like tax records, medical records, financial statements, and other files that you do not want someone using the same computer to see.

Creating an encrypted folder varies by operating system, and there are apps that create encrypted folders for you. To create simple created folders for your Microsoft Windows or Apple macOS computer:

Encrypted Folder on Windows 10

- **NOTE:** Make sure each computer user has their own logon. This process encrypts the folders on a per-user basis.
- Create a folder to act as your encrypted folder. Use a folder name that is not too obvious.
- Right-click on the folder and select "Properties".
- Click on "Advanced".
- Under the "Advanced Attributes" menu, check the box "Encrypt Contents and Secure Data".
- Clock "OK" then "Apply".
- Select "Apply changes to this folder, subfolders, and files", then click "OK".
- Be sure to Backup and password protect the encryption key.

Encrypted Folder for Apple macOS

- Open "Finder" then click on "Applications", then "Utilities".
- Open the "Disk Utility" app.
- Click on "File" > "New Image" > "Blank Image".
- In the "Save as" box, enter a name for your encrypted folder (without spaces). Don't make the name too obvious.
- In the "Name" sections, give the folder a common name.
- In the "Size" section, enter the anticipated folder size. Depending on the size of the files you want to protect, enter between "5 GB" and "25 GB". Remember that this folder will take up space on your hard drive.
- Under "Encryption", select "256 AES encryption".
- You will then be prompted to set a password for the encrypted folder. Please set a passphrase that you will not forget. If you forget it, the data is locked forever.
- Click "Save". The folder will be created in the form of a file.
- When you double-click on the newly created file, you will be prompted for the passphrase.
- After entering the passphrase, the encrypted folder will appear on your desktop. This encrypted folder appears and acts just like a USB drive on a Mac.
- Place the sensitive files in the encrypted folder, then right-click on the folder and select "Eject" to close it.

There are plenty of third-party apps available that allow you to easily encrypt either your entire computer or specific folders. I will not recommend one program over another, but please do your research before purchasing an app. The most important takeaway is that encrypting your computers, tablets, smartphones, and important files is critical to protecting your privacy. Some people don't like to think about the loss of their devices, but it is something they can plan for. The good news is that, very similar to privacy settings, you do not have to keep changing your encryption settings. Set it and forget it!

"ASK ME ANYTHING" ABOUT CYBER SECURITY AND PRIVACY

Implementation of the *Cyber Security Six Pack* ™ is a great way for everyone to increase their personal cyber protective profile, but it does not address all the questions I have been asked over the years. During his presentations, my favorite Chief Information Security Officer (CISO) had a segment at the end of the presentation called "Ask Me Anything." I adopted that practice for my teachings and presentations, and I want to share some of the most popular questions with you. Some of these questions require a 30-minute seminar to cover thoroughly, but I hope the brief responses answer the core of the questions.

Categories:

- The Internet
- Smartphones
- Phishing / Smishing / Social Engineering
- Home Computing
- Passwords and Multifactor / Two-Factor Authentication
- Email
- Web Browsing
- Home Networking
- Internet of Things (IoT)
- Virtual Private Networking (VPN)
- Privacy

The Internet

Q: What exactly is "The Internet"?

A: *Simply put, the Internet is a global network of computing and network devices that allow people to instantly communicate all over the world.*

Q: Who runs the Internet?

A: *No one person or country runs the Internet. Internet service providers around the globe manage vast networks that connect to each other, then charge individuals and companies to gain access.*

Q: What's the difference between the Internet, my home network, and Wi-Fi?

A: *The Internet is a global network of computing and network devices. Your home network connects all of your local computing devices to the global network. Wi-Fi is just a means to connect to your home network.*

Q: What is "The Cloud"?

A: *Somebody else's computer. :-) Storing your information "in the cloud" just means that it's saved on computers in a company's data center instead of yours. There is no central cloud. "The Cloud" sounds cooler than saying a data center in Montana.*

Q: Are the free social media sites like TikTok, Facebook and Instagram really free?

A: *There is no such thing as free when it comes to the Internet. If you are not paying cash for a service, you are paying by sharing information, which is monetized by the "free" service you are using.*

Q: Is it safe to go to the websites that offer in-theater movies for free?

A: *There is no such thing as "free", so you are paying for these movies with your personal information and your Internet bandwidth as the movie service proxies traffic through your Internet connection.*

Q: What is the "Dark Web" or the "Deep Web"?

A: *Even though the terms are sometimes used interchangeably, the Dark Web consists of searchable pages on the TOR (The Onion Network) network, an encrypted area of the Internet accessible only when using a special browser.*

The Deep Web consists of non-searchable pages on the TOR network that typically deal with illegal activity.

Q: Is the Internet really that dangerous?

A: *The Internet is like the American Wild West. A lot of building is going on, not a lot of governance in place, and plenty of bad guys. Know where to go, know where to stay clear of, and make sure that you know a good sheriff to help you deal with the bad guys.*

Q: How do I monitor my children on the Internet?

A: *There are plenty of apps available to monitor your children if the need arises. You should consult a cyber security professional to provide guidance on the specific computer, tablets, and smartphones you use. Not every app works on every device, so it's worth spending the money on a professional to make sure you have the monitoring you require.*

Smartphones

Q: Which is better – iPhones or Android smartphones?

A: *It depends on what you want to do with the smartphone and how much you want to pay. iPhones are more restrictive when it comes to installing apps and Android phones can be less expensive. It comes down to personal preference.*

Q: What's wrong with using a four-digit code to lock your smartphone?

A: *Using a four-digit code is better than using no code. Using a longer code or an alphanumeric password is more secure. As long as you do not use four consecutive numbers like "0000", it's ok.*

Q: Is fingerprint or facial recognition on a smartphone dangerous?

A: *It depends. Some manufacturers have very strong fingerprint and facial recognition systems, others not so much. Do your research before buying a device with these features.*

Q: Should I use banking apps on my smartphone?

A: *It depends on how you use your phone. You should never install banking apps on rooted or jailbroken smartphones. You should also avoid using banking apps if you install "free" versions of apps you normally pay for.*

Q: How many apps is too many apps?

A: *If you have so many apps that you are running out of space on your phone, you have too many apps. If you have not used an app in six months, close your account and delete the app.*

Q: What is jailbreaking an iPhone or "rooting" an Android phone?

Jailbreaking and rooting means that you are installing an alternative version of your smartphone's software. Some people do it to add more features to their device. You are taking a chance when you install alternative operating systems on your devices.

Q: How do I make my smartphone safer to use?

A: *There are several steps you can take to make a smartphone safer. There are several websites and books that can help. Start with turning on automatic updates, then use a VPN when using public Wi-Fi.*

Q: How do I protect my personal information when using a smartphone?

A: *Start with tightening up your privacy settings. There are literally dozens of settings that you can tweak to protect your information. Make sure that your smartphone is encrypted to protect your information in case it is lost or stolen.*

Q: How do I limit tracking when using a smartphone?

A: *There are location tracking and add tracking settings on every smartphone. Go online and learn how to limit or disable those settings on your particular device.*

Phishing / Smishing / Social Engineering

Q: What is Phishing?

A: *A phish is a fake email designed to get you to divulge personal information to compromise your device.*

Q: How do I tell if an email is a phish?

A: *It's not always easy. Start by checking the real "From" address carefully. If necessary, select "Forward" on the email and look at the "From" address there. Also, look for misspelled words, bad grammar, and if the message is alarming or urgent in tone. Bad actors try to scare you into action. Don't let the sense of urgency make you drop your guard.*

Q: I received an email from an online retailer stating that there was an unauthorized purchase on my account and should call a number or click on a link for more information. Should I contact them?

A: *Log into your retailer's account like you would normally, either through the mobile app or the website. Look for past orders to see if there are any messages from the retailer or any unauthorized orders. If there is something out of the ordinary, contact the retailer through the app or using the "Contact Us" area of the website. Never click on the links or use the phone numbers supplied in the email.*

Q: What is Smishing?

A: *A phishing message sent by SMS or text. If the message states that they are sending an update on a delivery, go to the retailer site or app for an update. Just because the message states it from a reputable delivery service does not make it true.*

Q: Are any links in text messages safe?

A: Don't click on links sent from an unknown person or company. It could take your smartphone browser to a site that could instantly compromise your smartphone.

Q: Should I respond to random text messages or ignore them?

A: Ignore them and block them. Curiosity killed the cat and compromised the smartphone.

Q: What is social engineering?

A: It is the art of convincing someone to give up confidential information. Bad actors call, text, and email people constantly, trying to manipulate them with one scary story or another. Your social security number was compromised – your computer has a virus and was detected by their system – your online retailer account has unauthorized purchases. They want the person to panic and provide whatever information is needed for them to compromise your account or identity.

Q: Is it safe to answer the calls from "Apple Support" or "Microsoft Support" as stated in CallerID?

A: No. These support teams typically don't initiate contact by phone. If the call is legitimate, they will leave a message with a contact email address or phone number. Look up the number or email address in a search engine to confirm.

Q: Should I call the toll-free numbers on the pop-up messages stating that my computer has a virus?

A: No. More than likely this is a scam in which the person you call will ask you to install a program to connect to your computer to look for the problem – complete scam. If your computer has up-to-date anti-virus software on it, one of their messages will pop-up if you have a virus. If you do not have up-to-date anti-virus software, purchase a third-party Internet security suite, install it and scan for problems. If there is really a virus, the new suite will clean it up. Additionally, never install remote access software on your computer from any company, even from companies you normally do business with – insist on a technician to talk you through the problem.

Home Computing

Q: Which computer operating system is better – Apple macOS, Microsoft Windows, ChromeOS, or Linux?

A: *Depends. Your computer should be selected based on your requirements. You want to use the operating system that meets your requirements. If all you want is a web browser and email, you could get by with a Chromebook. If you need something with a lot of RAM that runs a variety of different applications, you may need Windows. Purchase based on your budget and needs, not popularity.*

Q: Which pop-up alerts should I believe, and which should I ignore?

Never click on pop-up alerts. If your anti-virus software sends a pop-up message, close the pop-up alert and open the full program. If the pop-up alert was legitimate, you will see it in the full program as well.

Q: I'm buying a new computer. How much RAM do I need? What size hard drive?

A: *Depends (I say this a lot). Buy the RAM and hard drive size needed for your requirements. Extra RAM and hard drive storage is always a plus.*

Q: Do I need to update my printer like I update my computer and smartphone?

A: *If your printer connects to the network, yes it needs to be updated. If it is on the network, it is subject to attack, so at a minimum the security updates should be applied.*

Q: Do I need to pay to renew my Internet Security Suite?

A: *Yes. When the suite expires, you no longer receive updates against the newest threat. If the renewal fee seems high, email the company and negotiate for a better price. If they do not offer a better price, find a new internet security suite with equal (or better) features and switch.*

Q: How often should I Backup my computer?

A: *Depends* ☺ *. If you process critical information on your computer daily, back it up daily at the end of the day or use a service that backs it up constantly and stores it on a drive or in the cloud. If you do not process critical information regularly, once every week or two is fine.*

Q: Should I encrypt my computer's hard drive?

A: *If you have a laptop and travel with it – absolutely. If you have a desktop and have sensitive information or pictures on your computer – absolutely. If you do not have sensitive information on the computer and encrypting the hard drive does not severely impact the computer's performance – absolutely.*

Q: *Does all of this security slow my computer down?*

A: *Every security app you install will have some impact on the computer. Most modern security suites run very efficiently, so while the computer startup may take a few seconds (not minutes) more, you should experience no perceivable slowdown of computer performance if you use a reputable security suite.*

Q: How often should I purchase a new computer, smartphone, or tablet?

A: *Depends (I know - I can't help it). If your computer is performing everything that you need to do with it, I would not purchase a new one until support ends on the current operating systems. You should replace any computer, tablet or smartphone that can no longer be patched.*

Passwords and Multifactor Authentication

Q: Which is stronger – a password or a passphrase?

A: *A passphrase is typically longer and stronger and not subject to a dictionary-style attack.*

Q: How often should I change my password/passphrase?

A: *Any password that deals with money (banking, investing, cryptocurrency), should be changed once a year at a minimum. It is a good practice to change both important passwords and fire detector batteries on Daylight Saving Time days.*

Q: Do I really need to use unique passphrases on my online accounts?

A: *Yes, yes, and yes again. If your passphrase is compromised by criminal hackers, they will use tools to try that same passphrase on hundreds of online services. If you use the same passphrase everywhere, the compromise of one site quickly becomes the compromise of three, four, or more sites.*

Q: How do I remember dozens of unique passwords for dozens of online accounts?

A: *Use passphrases. A passphrase base uses the first letter of each word in a sentence from your favorite song, poem or other document instead of the variation of a standard word. Add a simple suffix related to the online service name to the first part of the passphrase and you have it.*

Q: Is it safe to save usernames and passwords in a browser?

A: *No. This information is easily exposed to anyone using the same computer. If you want to automatically have your information filled in to save time at login, purchase a password manager app.*

Q: What is multifactor authentication?

A: *When you are logging in using your username and password, multi factor authentication requires you to provide a code or approve an app notification before the login is complete. That means that even if a criminal actor steals your username and password, they still cannot complete the login to your account without the code.*

Q: Which is safer for multi factor authentication – text, email, or smartphone app?

A: *Smartphone app, text, then email – in that order.*

Q: Are password managers secure?

A: *As long as you purchase a password manager from a reputable company and use it properly, it should be safe.*

Q: How do I know if my password has been exposed somewhere?

A: *Go to https://haveibeenpwned.com to see if your email address was associated with a breach. The sites will tell you if passwords were exposed.*

Email

Q: Should I use the email address provided by my Internet Service Provider (ISP)?

A: *If you move and change ISPs, all of the accounts associated with that email address may be lost. Better to purchase a low-cost email account or register your own name as a domain and create a really cool email address.*

Q: Which free email service is best?

A: *I cannot recommend one "free" service over another because nothing is truly free. Some "free" services scan your email and send you targeted ads based on the content of your email. Read the terms of service for all free accounts and measure that against low-cost email accounts.*

Q: What is a secure email system?

A: A secure email system is an email system that provides more traditional securities than any traditional email systems. For example, secure email systems can encrypt sensitive documents and pictures. Therefore, they can only be seen by the intended recipient.

Q: How do I get a custom email address with my name as the domain, like john@smith.com?

A: Many popular domain registration companies offer low-cost or free custom email addresses with the purchase of a domain. It may be hard to find a domain like "smith.com" available, using your full name may work.

Q: Should I have more than one email address?

A: Definitely. Most people have at least two (personal and work/school). You should have separate email addresses to keep your
really important electronic correspondence separate from electronic correspondence related to other online accounts like food accounts.

Q: How do I stop someone from tracking me in an email?

A: Go into your email app settings and disable the automatic display of graphics. Companies track email messages by inserting tracking images so small that you do not see them. Disabling graphics shuts that down.

Q: How do I block spam and phishing messages?

A: *Adjust the spam and malware settings in your email app to be more restrictive. Some third-party Internet security suites offer extra protection against spam and phishing.*

Q: What is an email archive?

A: *If you have years (or decades) of email that you want to save in a safe place, you can create an email archive and export those messages to a single file. This is a great way of preserving email related to a special event like a wedding or a birth.*

Web Browser

Q: Which web browser is best?

A: *Any browser that meets your requirements is best. Make sure that the browser is regularly patched and updated. Make sure that the browser has a private mode and does not collect your browsing information for sale.*

Q: What is "Private" mode in a browser?

A: *Normally, web browsers retain information like your browsing history, search records and cookies until you manually delete it.*
Private Mode browsing only keeps that information if the browser is in use.

Q: Which browser does not share your information?

A: *There are a few browsers that focus on privacy. Do your online research to find the right one for you.*

Q: Should I use more than one browser?

A: *It is a good idea to use more than one browser. One browser that is compatible with most websites and a second browser that focuses on privacy. If you cannot visit a site with your privacy-focused browser, use the other one.*

Q: What are browser add-ons and extensions?

A: *A software addition that adds features to your browser.*

Q: Are browser add-ons and extensions safe?

A: Many browser add-on and extensions offer minimal features but gain a lot of personal information from your web browsing. Only use add-ons and extensions from reputable companies.

Q: How many tabs is "too many" tabs?

A: When you log into a website and you are not in private mode, each tab can access that site as if it was the tab used to log in. If you log into your bank, you should not open any other tabs. That said, if you are logged into any site, keep the tabs to a minimum. If you are not logged into anything, have fun.

Q: Can someone really see my saved passwords in a browser if they have access to my computer?

A: Absolutely. It's easy, but I'm not going to teach you to hack in this book. Use a search engine to find a video about it. You will never save passwords in a browser again.

Q: Which search engine is the best?

A: It depends. Do you want the most information returned during a search or do you want to search without that information being used to send you ads? Do your research and figure out what features make you the most comfortable when searching.

Home Networking

Q: What is an Internet Service Provider (ISP)?

A: An ISP is the company that provides your connection to the Internet.

Q: How do I protect my home router?

A: There are several steps to keep your router protected. Start with backing up the router, then updating it. Make sure that your Wi-Fi networks are using WPA2 encryption or better. Turn on any firewall features and turn off remote administration. Make sure you change the default password on the router.

Q: How often should I update my home router?

A: If automatic updates are not available, check for updates once a month.

Q: What is the guest network on my home router?

A: A guest network allows someone to use your Wi-Fi but not access any of the devices on your home network. If someone outside of your family has access to your Wi-Fi, enable the guest network and have them use that instead.

Q: What is a home network DMZ (demilitarized zone)?

A: Some routers have a DMZ, or demilitarized zone, that does not have the same protections as the home network. Traffic to this zone of the home router is faster, but it's more susceptible to a home attack. This is a good zone for video game consoles that want to decrease lag.

Q: Can I create a DMZ on my home network?

A: You can create a DMZ on your home router, but if you do not have networking experience, you may inadvertently expose your network to attack. It is better to buy a router with a built-in DMZ port.

Q: How can I limit connections to my home network?

A: Most routers have a feature called MAC Address Filtering that can be used to limit access to your Wi-Fi.

Q: How can I tell if an unauthorized person is using my network?

A: Unless your router has a logging feature and you regularly read those logs, it is hard to tell if someone is on the network. The best way to find out is to change the Wi-Fi password and wait to see who complains.

Q: How often should I change my Wi-Fi passwords?

A: It depends on who has the password. If you have a party and give all of the guests the password, you should change the password right after the party. If you are not sure, change your password on Daylight Savings Day.

The Internet of Things (IoT)

Q: What is the Internet of Things (IoT)?

A: If a device connects to the Internet but is not a traditional piece of computer equipment (desktop, laptop, tablet, smartphone, printer, router, firewall), it is considered IoT.

Q: What are some examples of IoT?

A: Smart TVs, Wi-Fi-connected security cameras, doorbells, locks, gaming consoles, kitchen appliances with Wi-Fi connections, digital assistants, smartwatches, Wi-Fi-connected security systems and thermostats.

Q: Are IoT devices more susceptible to hacking?

A: Many IoT devices are not patched or updated. Those devices are more susceptible to hacking because discovered vulnerabilities are never fixed.

Q: Do I need to update my IoT devices? If so, how often?

A: You should definitely update your IoT devices. You should check for updates once a month.

Q: Is it true that criminal hackers can see what is on my internet-connected home cameras?

A: There have been reports that criminal hackers have gained access to home cameras. Any external connection to your IoT devices should require multi-factor authentication.

Q: If my Wi-Fi goes down, does that impact my security cameras and security systems?

A: If you have a Wi-Fi-based security system, it will be impacted when the Wi-Fi goes down. Make sure your system has a telephone backup or still provides some level of functionality when Wi-Fi goes down.

Q: Do I have to open "ports" on my router to make my IoT device work?

A: You should not have to open ports on your router for your IoT devices. If you must open ports on your router to make your IoT device work, I would look for a different device.

Q: Do digital assistant devices compromise my privacy?

A: It depends on the device. Some devices listen to your every word until it hears a keyword and then starts saving the conversation. Check with your manufacturer for details on privacy.

Q: Do IoT devices require extra security?

A: IoT devices have the same level of security attention as your computer or smartphone. IoT devices must have a secure configuration and should be patched regularly.

Virtual Private Networking (VPN)

Q: What exactly is VPN?

A: Virtual Private Networking (VPN) creates an encrypted line of communication (aka VPN Tunnel) between your device and your VPN provider or target VPN endpoint.

Q: How does VPN protect your information?

A: By hiding your communications in encrypted tunnels, the VPN prevents the people that run public Wi-Fi hotspots from seeing (and selling) your information.

Q: Is VPN legal?

A: VPN is legal in most countries. If you travel to other countries, be sure to check the laws on VPN before you enable it.

Q: Does the average person need VPN?

A: VPN is a great tool to have in your computer, tablet, and smartphone toolbox.

Q: Does VPN make me untraceable?

A: VPN does not make you untraceable, but it can change where websites think you are operating from.

Q: When should I use VPN?

A: If you are using Wi-Fi outside of the home or office, you should use VPN.

Q: Is free VPN safe?

A: Anything "free" has a cost. It's typically your information that will be sold in exchange for using the service. Do your research on the free VPN services. It is better to pay a few dollars a month for a service that you know does not sell your information.

Q: Does VPN slow down my connection?

A: VPN will indeed slow down your connection. How much it slows down your connection depends on the service, how many connection points the service has, what service point you are connecting to, and how many people are on the network. For instance, if you live in Boston and your VPN provider has a connection point in Boston, the impact will be minimal. If the closest connection point is in Virginia, the connection speed will naturally be slower.

Q: Why do some sites and online services block VPN?

A: VPN disguises who you really are, and some websites and services don't like that. For example, some online movie services are licensed to play certain movies in certain countries and not in others. If you connect to a VPN from another country, you will have access to different movies and may violate the licensing terms for the company.

Privacy

Q: What is "privacy" as it pertains to computers and the Internet?

A: The activities associated with keeping your personal information free from observation and interception.

Q: Is privacy dead?

A: Not dead, but not exactly healthy. People have become comfortable sharing all sorts of information online, especially social media. This information is being sold and people are comfortable with that as well. Privacy is just viewed differently these days.

Q: Are there laws that protect our privacy on the Internet?

A: There are a variety of layers that protect information on the Internet. Some laws govern how information is stored and protected. Some laws limit what information is collected. If you want to know more about the laws that impact your country and/or state, investigate online.

Q: Am I required to use accurate name, address, and birthdate information on the Internet?

A: Absolutely not. You can create online accounts with the same name but use different addresses and birthdate information. This makes it harder (but not im-

possible) for the people that collect this data to form profiles about you. Unfortunately, some people create online accounts with completely false information and lure people into online relationships. It's called "catfishing." Not illegal.

Q: Are there services that help protect privacy online?

A: There are several services that provide that service. There are also services that help when your privacy has been violated and personal (or unflattering) information about you has been distributed on the Internet. Do your research to find the service that is right for you.

Q: How do I protect the private information of my children?

A: Any computing device used by your children should have parental controls enabled and the parents should monitor for any violations. You should also talk to your child about maintaining their private information and the private information of the family. Ensuring your child is not oversharing information is now a critical parental responsibility.

Q: How do I protect my privacy while traveling?

A: Back up all your devices before traveling. Make sure that your devices are encrypted in case they are lost or stolen. Make sure that all of your devices are updated and patched before you leave. Ensure that your security software is updated and active. Use VPN when using Wi-Fi in the hotel or any other place while traveling.

Q: What do I do if my privacy is violated online?

A: Contact the website that violated your privacy and ask them to take the information down. Engage a service that specializes in reputation defense. Contact a lawyer.

PACKING IT ALL UP

———————————

Now that you have completed this book, you should feel more confident in your knowledge of personal cyber security and your ability to protect your devices and privacy better. While what you learned is just the tip of the iceberg of the massive world of cyber security, you are now more cyber aware than the average person, which gives you an advantage over the criminal hackers out there.

You learned some essential information related to cyber security and privacy:

- You discovered the parallels between cyber security and physical security.

- You learned a few hard truths about the vulnerabilities existing in all computing devices and that mitigations are required to stay safe.

- You learned about the different types of criminal hackers operating today and the cyber security professionals that work to keep them at bay.

- You learned about the difference between a virus, a worm, and other forms of malware.

- You learned about the types of attacks the criminal hackers use to compromise computers and people.

95

Most importantly, we learned that cyber security is not rocket science. Applying protection to your digital devices that connect to the Internet (and each other) does not require an advanced degree or an affinity for electronic devices. It does not matter whether you are a young person setting up their first smartphone or an older person using digital devices for many years. Everyone using a computer, tablet, or smartphone can take a few small steps to increase personal cyber security and privacy significantly. Well, six simple steps.

- <u>Use Unique Passphrases and Multi-Factor Authentication for your Online Accounts</u>

   Applying unique passphrases and MFA to your online accounts is not hard and is worth the effort.

- <u>Back Up Your Computers, Tablets, and Smartphones Regularly</u>

   It does not matter what method you choose, as long as you choose an action and regularly back up your devices.

- <u>Keep Operating Systems and Applications Updated</u>

   Just like changing the oil in a car, updating and patching your electronic devices is something you must do regularly, or there will be problems.

- <u>Install and Maintain a Third-Party Internet Security Suite</u>

Using a security suite is a textbook case of an ounce of prevention being worth a pound of cure.

- Limit Access to Personal Information (Location, Browsing History, etc.)

  Limiting access to your personal information is a shared responsibility, but most of the responsibility is on you.

- Encrypt Your Computer, Tablet, Smartphone, and Important Files

  Encrypting your computers, tablets, smartphones, and important files is critical to protecting your privacy.

Many more techniques, tricks, and tips are available to secure your digital devices further. Some steps are easy, while some measures are much more advanced. Some of the step-by-step instructions provided earlier in the book may change as devices are updated, and operating systems evolve. Please research the settings for your specific devices and operating systems online to ensure you have the latest instructions.

This book's goal is to make you safer than the average person when it comes to protecting your electronic devices and privacy. Through definition, explanation, and demonstration, the hope is that you are encouraged to implement the recommendations in this book. It is also a hope that you share this information with others so that they too can become a harder target. It's us against the bad actors. Let's all outrun the bear together.

Acknowledgements

There are too many people to thank for their support over the years, but I will try:

Alice, Frank, Vivian, Chuck, Tammy, Tiara, Daniel, Stephanie, Anson, Aiden, Daheen, Lashanda, Veronica, Lisa, Obsidian, Jasmine, Alicia, Charles, Mary, Ben, Sue, Bernice, Vermell, Pam, Dianne, Joseph, Arlene, Dottie, Rozzie, Rochelle, Malik, India, Markie, Niecey, Sue, Glenn, Gerrie, Neil, Consuela, Del, Debby, Ron, Keith, Denita, Rodney, Diane, Jonathan, Ryan, Al, Neeta, Julie, Jane, Charu, Walter, Matt, Miguel, Aldo, Frank, Joe, Esther, Demark, Brent, Kingsley, Yolanda, Julie, Adrian, Nick, Beau, Dan, Malcolm, Narith, Serafin, Trena, Charwin, Rick, David, Gus, Tarek, Gerry, Nicole, Kaz, Carlos, Sarah, James, Johnny, Joyce, Liz, Fiona, Val, Annette, Mary, Bobo, Sandy, Melody, Mike, Sophia, Natasha, Sherwin, Rochelle, Sharlene, Steve, Brian, Brie, Ken, Kris, Melissa, Jennifer, Sergio, Roman, Tovar, Kim, Sparks, China, Star, Jeff, Powell, Shy, Pat, Jose, Viviana, Makira, Alex, Dawn, Loretta, Gabby, Ron, Stephen, Jamison, Faheem, Kendra, Roy, Linda, Kelvin, Karla, Mamie, Mamie Lynn, Marvin, Mary, Donna, Keith, Winston, Deborah, Marlese, Anna, Belquise, Jodian, Amateka, Paul, Jatae, William, Ellen, Kelvin, Amy, Haley, Kamoya, Juan, Fehintola, Harith, Gregory, Angel, Ignatius, Kamoya, Dawn, Derek, Doug, Carmen, Joe, Nikki, Denise, Z, Gary, Frank, Locksley, Yohanna, Herbie, Jason, Charwin, Lonnie, Pam, Dedra, Georgia, Chaunte', Rock, Stacy, David, Tamela, Reginald, and all of our neighborhood parents that kept us in line like great parents do. Last, but definitely not least, I want to thank my Lord and Savior Jesus Christ – my light, my strength, my song. If your name is not on this list, don't be offended. Charge it to my head, not my heart.

ABOUT THE AUTHOR

James Patterson "Pat" Wicks is a cyber security executive with over 30 years of experience configuring and protecting computers, smartphones, networks, and other electronic devices. He also has 24 years of experience as a technology instructor at a major university in New York City. A self-described "cyber security evangelist," Pat Wicks has achieved several technology certifications over the years and speaks publicly about the need to secure our personal and corporate information systems. Brooklyn-born and southern-reared, Pat Wicks is a veteran of the United States Army (Hooah!), a doting husband, proud father of two, loving son, allegedly amusing brother, and supportive member of his extensive extended family.

LEGAL DISCLAIMER

Information obtained for this book has been obtained using various sources including my intellectual property obtained during my 24+ years of experience in the cyber security field. The *Cyber Security Six Pack* ™ was created just for you!

While some information, such as steps to secure an IPhone is public information, I do not attempt to circumvent or replace any instructions that the manufacturer provides to its consumers. Whenever possible or appropriate, seek the user manual for your devices. The intent of this manual is to simplify where possible, and create a space where protecting your information is comfortable and easy.

Made in United States
North Haven, CT
13 August 2022